Flashcuts Out of Chaos

Flashcuts Out of Chaos

Poems by Charles W. Brice

WordTech Editions

Published by WordTech Editions
P.O. Box 541106
Cincinnati, OH 45254-1106

ISBN: 978-1-62549-181-7

Poetry Editor: Kevin Walzer
Business Editor: Lori Jareo

Visit us on the web at www.wordtechweb.com

Cover art: Richard Claraval, "Ignudo 17,"
richardclaravalcontemporaryfigurativedrawingssculpture.com

For Judy

All that talk about love and this *is what that word was pointing at.*
—Tony Hoagland

Table of Contents

Include a Brief Biographical Statement (Three Lines) with
Your Poetry Submission

I. The Inverted World

II. Wild Pitch

III. Milliseconds of Mystery

Include a Brief Biographical Statement (Three Lines) with Your Poetry Submission

I am a sixty-year-old man and look it.
My once auburn beard is grey,
my Beatle hair all gone now. I have

this awful stomach. At first
I thought I was distended,
bloated from some disease or other

only to discover that I'm fat. That's
too many lines. I'll try again:
I'm a sixty-year-old former psychoanalyst—

no, the editor might hate Freud,
or maybe she had a bad analysis;
I know I did—twice.

Better try something else:
I'm sixty years old and have a PhD
in psychology. That won't work,

maybe the editor hates PhDs.
Maybe she became an editor
because some English professor

told her she couldn't write.
That's why she's sitting at a desk
with 500 poems to read by midnight.

Here, this should do it: I'm a sixty-
year-old freelance writer living
in Pittsburgh. Wait, it's probable

an 18-year-old pimply-brained
freshman honor student is reading
this first cut of poems. He's been rejected

by every journal he's submitted poems to
because…because old farts like me
get published instead of him.

So he'll pass on Mr. Geriatric. Okay,
fine, let's drop the age thing:
I'm a freelance writer in Pittsburgh

who attends the writing program
at the University of Pittsburgh. Well,
not really. While I've taken several

writing courses at Pitt, even a couple
graduate workshops in writing,
the only times I'm in the writing program

are when I'm partying at Grady's,
watching him smoke a couple Js,
wishing I could join him (I get bronchial

spasms when I toke), or talking to his students,
the real writers, while they can still stand
up. Goddammit, maybe this will fly:

I'm a freelance writer in Pittsburgh.
Wait, "freelance writer," that's code
for "old fart." Mr. 18-year-old

first reader will see through that
faster than a priest grabs
an altar boy after Mass.

Okay, last try: I'm a, um...
hell, I'm Pittsburgh. Thanks,
yinz, for reading my poems.

I. The Inverted World

There is the question of whether life is long enough to get over anything.
—Jim Harrison

Marmalade

The porter with his tiny xylophone
calls passengers to breakfast or dinner,
waiters in the dining car, white coats,
careful articulation of the breakfast
fare, shiny, sterling silverware—
rhythmic clatter of cups and saucers,
boxcar acrobats balance huge trays
as the train sways and heaves.
That first taste of marmalade
scooped from a serving boat
with a tiny silver spoon.
Those fine black men make
a fuss over my toast and tea.
How did they regard us—
three fat pink people
who boarded in Cheyenne
and headed to Omaha in 1954?
They made us feel like the queen,
king, and crown prince of breakfast,
and helped us forget that none of them
could travel the train as passengers,
or stay in any hotel along our route.
Centuries of indignities scattered
across the tracks, our offal ravaged
in the train's turbulent wake.
Something about the gap between that first step
into the Pullman car and the track
came after me at night for years.

Jesus' Mother Didn't Have Blond Hair

Jesus never made it to Europe.
—Amiri Baraka

There was the smell of Sister Marino's white
habit, something beyond clean, beyond pure
even. There was the hard wooden seat that
folded up and then down again, the cold
metal siding in the design of vines
and leaves, and the solid, unmovable legs
screwed fast to the floor, the desktop
with a well on the right—for what?—
not big enough for a cup.

There was her voice, shrill and black
as the grotto-hood that framed her head
and made her look like a saint
carved in marble. She passed out
fancy colored paper and crayons.
"Draw a picture of Mary," she said.
I'd only scribbled before this. Everyone
got right to work: tiny knocks
from the kid's crayons
as their Marys found form.

Who's Mary? I wondered. My drawing
was of some lady in rags, with the kinky
black hair of Mrs. Dee, my kindergarten
teacher in the public school. My mother
had promised God that she'd send me
to St. Mary's Catholic school if my bone
marrow test came out negative. I was saving
her soul. Everyone but me drew Mary with silky
blond hair and dressed her in the finest robes.
My picture, drawn on that first day of first
grade, was the only one Sister Marino
didn't put on the bulletin board.

I think now of Sister Marino, a bride

of Christ condemned to a dusty
little hole in the prairie like Cheyenne.
For her nothing worked out. I can still hear
her "tsk" as she looked at my raggedy Madonna.
Couldn't she at least have had a classroom
of kids who knew what Mary looked like?

Daydream

Those cottonwoods were thrilling,
they danced like ballerinas,
and sometimes went mad
throwing their white blazon
all over the city like furry confetti.

"He daydreams," my mother
read aloud Sister Susanna's
terse and torrid critique.
"What's a daydream?" I asked.
"It's when you look out the window
and stop listening in class,"
my mother said.

But the music I heard/
saw out that window:
The Nutcracker Suite—
elephants skittered like leaves
across the sky, Jesus jumped
from his cross and chased
Lazarus to life.

Someone picked up the end
of a river and found frogs
reciting the Baltimore Catechism.
Streets rolled up into concrete
spirals like the toffee we bought
in Jackson Hole.

"Don't daydream," my mother said.
Sister Susanna, so gray, read
everything to us third graders
out of a black book packed
with prayers, pleas, and
purposelessness.

Out the window she danced
like a sailor, wore a parakeet

on her shoulder, a patch
over one eye—Sister Long
Joan Silver yelled,
"Ahoy, matey," and swilled gallons
of rum while the St. Mary's Marching Band
played Mussorgsky, "The Great Gate of Kiev."

"Stop daydreaming," my mother said.

Goodbye

Auntie Ursal would sing to me, or chant
her rosary beads, rattle them against my bed,
during what seemed, in seven-year-old time,
unending nosebleeds. Later we'd hop

a bus. Ten cents got you anywhere in Cheyenne.
She'd take me to the Mayflower Restaurant on 17th Street
where the marinara sauce atop my spaghetti
allowed a first taste of garlic, and where

she showed me holy cards her son, Terry,
had won during twelve years of Catholic education.
Cousin Terry, who once told me that Marines,
like him, were so tough they jumped out of airplanes

without parachutes. Terry commanded tanks
in Korea and, when drunk, relived his worst
times there. He once threw a drink at a friend
in our basement, then collapsed in tears. He

was in Korea again where (the Chinese
about to attack) one of his men mired in quicksand
pled for his life. They'd run out of time. Terry
threw him a morphined syringe and said goodbye,

as did we to Terry one hot June morning in 1957.
He'd run off the road near Torrington. Auntie Ursal
jerked at the 21-gun salute and touched his flag-
draped coffin. His brother Marines looked sharp.

At Ten I Thought Everyone Had A Shoebox Filled With Human Teeth And Seashells

Hemingway was either drunk
or writing, a bore, no fun at all,
or so say the few I've met who knew
him. For me he was Papa, a man
who took me fishing in Cuba,
gun running in Martinique,
Civil War fighting in Spain,
drinking and whoring in France,
and big game hunting in Africa.
He taught me how to love a woman

more than war, and how to walk defeated,
but never destroyed, along an infinite path
of grief. He even taught me how to end it—
decisively, simply, and with grace. Some people
loved my real father, a round man in a brown suit
who cried for days when his brother
Francis died from the same excesses
that would claim my father in later years.
At ten I thought everyone had a shoebox

filled with human teeth and seashells. My dad
spent WWII in the Evacuation Corps
where the unspeakable stifled explanation
of those polished surfaces—teeth pulled
from the mouths of Japanese soldiers
that my pudgy childhood fingers found
amid craggy shells from Guadalcanal. My father

smiled often, had a grateful laugh, and avoided
any brand of toil other than lifting a bourbon glass
to his lips. He spent his life drinking and watching
the Ed Sullivan Show. Hungry when drunk,
he'd fry and burn an egg, then another,
to brim his empty mass, his booze-bloated
corpse to be. What is the nothingness

that nothing fills? He never wrote anything
save his name, rather elaborately, on bar tabs.
The only similarities to Papa were the boxing
he did in WWII and the desperate drinking.
I wasn't his son; I was an excuse, a conduit
to a Fleischmann's Bourbon bottle,
the glass tit that ran his life and ours.

Don't Try[1]

1. K.O.

My father believed in kindness, Count Basie,
and Sergeant Bilko. My dad: drooping Buddha
eyelids, wilted right hand, clinging to an asbestos-
packed, Micronite filtered, Kent cigarette. My mother

pounded on his chest and screamed, "You
drunken sot; you stupid son of a bitch!" stopping
only after dad bear-hugged her into weariness.
Once, in Jackson Hole, Wyoming, he broke her nose.
Its crack still echoes and thrills. My job was to end

this war. I'd drive them down Requiem Highway
'til my father stopped drinking, or my mother,
preoccupied with me, forgot to smell his breath.
We'd pass the town of No Bottles In Brown Bags,
spend the night where no cocktail waitress splayed

atop a bar above my father who could barely
raise his head for a peek. We'd find a ZZ chapter:
a no-step program for daddy, and send him
to non-meetings. But on the way we were stopped

by the Reality Patrol. I was cited, tried, and convicted
for driving under the influence of bombast and
grandiosity. I, their Designated Redeemer, had fallen
off the wagon, had failed them by becoming me.

2. Echo

Outside the Wort Hotel
In Jackson Hole, Wyoming
I hang by my knees upside
Down from a steel railing

In the Wort's Silver Dollar Bar
My mom and dad drink

23

And drink and drink and drink and drink
That night
That night my mother beats
On my father's chest and arms
Calls him an asshole
A drunken sop

He breaks her nose with one punch
Its crack still echoes
Next day outside the Wort Hotel
I hang from that steel railing

The inverted world looks good

Prematurely Ripped

My mother often rampaged our house naked,
a hideous red-lumped scar jagged across her
abdomen, incised to prepare my arrival.
"Your head was so perfect," she told me over
and over, "you were a Caesarian section,"
and marrowed my understanding of everything.

Other babies born the usual way had heads
twisted and pointy, like my friend Joe whose dome
had a point, but who was my best friend anyway.
They named me Charles Ward Brice, Junior,
after my dad, of course, who went by Ward.
He had been the youngest in his family. His

sisters named him after a paperboy on whom
they had crushed. My dad's father was Charles
Otis Brice. Thank god I was never Charles Otis Brice, III.
(Remember Otis from Mayberry, the town drunk
who immured himself with his own key?)
In the marching band at St. Mary's they called me

Barley Chise—better than Butterball and Fatso,
my playground monikers in that school of Christ.
I disliked Barley almost as much as Charles—
so formal—but not as much as Ward—so weird.
On our Christmas cards one year my mother glued
my newborn perfect head over a photo of my father's

head, and my father's crusty face upon my infant
picture—a palimpsest of perfidy that, years later,
awoke my near comatose analyst—almost.

I Never Got Over the Rabbits and the Badger

Clouds dapple the Wyoming sky,
Punctuate nothingness, like rocks
In a Zen garden. Wind sears
The prairie, enforces no-mind—
The sun, a vicious hunter,
From which no one can hide.

Joe and I played with his .22 rifle
While our parents drank
And played gin rummy
After WYO football games.
We were 10 years old.

One time two rabbits, noses busy,
Graybellies soft and inviting,
Sat back and looked at us,
Curious about two boys
Walking their land on a sunny,
Windy, Wyoming day.

The rabbits jumped and quivered
When I gut-shot them.
They hadn't known I was a fat
Blond boy named Death.

Nine years later Joe and I
Sat on a boulder smoking a joint
At his dad's ranch near Buford.
We took turns shooting his .22 at
A badger. Pinned outside his cave,
He'd probably been hunting gopher,
Or out to feel the tempered breeze,
Sun warming his downy fur.

The gun scope malfunctioned:
I think I wounded him. Some
Granite ricocheted into his eye.

Last night I was called in a dream
To help execute my brother-in-law.
I sat across from him on a couch.
He wanted to die by firing squad.

I was one of three shooters.
Maybe I'll have the blank, I hoped.

My brother-in-law's grim smile—
We'd all be locked and loaded.

That's a horrible way to die, I said.
But it's what he wanted.

I awake and understand, finally,
The absurd idea of a benevolent God.

So Important

It was so important to fold your hands
in an upright position while serving
Mass. Father Mac insisted on this

configuration of fingers and hands.
This was what your hands would do
when they weren't pouring wine or water

over the trembling fingers of Father Mac
who drank too much wine and not enough
water, kept his fingers crossed

over the chalice waiting for us to pour more
wine. And now these years later
I know my perfect masses were the means

not to think about my mother screaming
at my father that she wanted a divorce
and wished him dead. My father,

the sweetest drunk ever, sat
in his green chair and laughed
at Phil Silvers and never spoke to me

of anything more significant than
to say I shouldn't shave too high
up on my cheekbones.

Wild Turkey

Mad Ireland hurt you into poetry.
—W.H. Auden on W.B Yeats

Five years old and ill with Rheumatic Fever
I spent hours watching robins pull
night crawlers from our front lawn.

Sometimes they lingered over their prey,
skittery as the worm wiggled
in their mouths, making me think

of trying to eat brown spaghetti
while riding a merry-go-round.
So, when Sister Humbert announced

that we were to draw a bird
in sixth grade art class, I was elated.
I loved this cranky nun who often lost

her temper, once slamming a book down
on her desk so hard the glass top broke.
Now I'd please her. I'd draw a robin that

would make St. Francis weep and chuckle.
But my robin was impaired: it had no neck,
she said, and after my third try, she threw it

in the garbage, as she did my heart the day
she awarded the statue of St. Francis I'd given her
for Christmas to our class spelling bee champ.

Sister Humbert hated that I was an only child.
To this proud and angry woman, one of six
children, an only child was as spoiled as

a neckless robin with a fetid breast. Sister
Humbert never met an opinion she didn't express;
chattered so much that old Doc Ryan once

cemented her mouth shut during a root canal,
or so he claimed ('course his favorite bird
and the anesthesia he preferred was Wild Turkey).

But now I thank that nettled nun and her psalm
of scorn. The nail she drove into my artistic palm
hurt me into poetry, and festers gladly still.

My First Poetry Teacher

If she liked you, Sister Humbert would
pull out her pen and draw a red check
mark on your cheek, grab that cheek
between thumb and forefinger, and
shake it back and forth until you screamed.

When you angered her she'd wrap fifteen
decades of rosary around your throat and tug,
or cold-cock you as she did Ronnie Davis
one frigid Cheyenne morning when he
pushed through a crowd of girls to get into our
classroom and its promised warmth.

She knocked Ronnie on his ass with a hard right
to the nose. People crossed themselves while
Ronnie rose up like some sixth grade god and
landed one to her gut. She fell like a huge
cottonwood strewn with Halloween toilet tissue.
The clangor of rosary beads when she hit the tile
made Hector's fallen armor sound silent and inglorious.

She made us memorize poems that year.
Mine was Longfellow's, "Excelsior!"
Some young Alpine buck climbed a
mountain pass even though a wise old
peasant warned him not to, and a maiden
offered him her breasts for a pillow, an
image that electrified my eleven year old
mind. People crossed themselves, but they
found him dead in the snow the next day:
"There in the twilight, cold and gray,
lifeless but beautiful he lay," was Longfellow's
description, which also described Sister
Humbert's Dominican habit, with its black
grotto hood and white scapular, and Ronnie's
face as she led him away from us forever.

What She Held—1966

Foot-stomping cold
on that frozen platform
in Cheyenne, she waited
for her husband's train.
He was an engineer. She
only saw him once or twice
a month. He had to watch
the tracks, couldn't take his eyes
off them even for a second.
He'd slide his hand out the cab
window as his diesel zoomed by.

I was waiting for my grandpa
from Omaha. Grandpa liked
to spread himself over both seats
in the coach car. He bathed rarely
and ate a garlic bulb at his seat,
often winning for himself alone
an entire railroad car. I heard
a roar and felt a rumble
as a train pulled into the depot—
not my grandpa's train,
not her husband's train—

icicles decorated this engine.
Some guy waved his cowboy
hat out a window, railroad workers
yelled yahoo! Snow kicked up
into frostclouds like a crystal
dream. Ride 'em cowboy! I yelled,
and cheered this triumph
over the savage Wyoming winter.
I dreamed back a hundred years—
we lacked only a steam engine—
privileged to see something this real.

After that train left, the woman
and I stomped around some more

on our icy platform. Soon
rumble and roar renewed,
an engine parted the frost
and a gloved hand eased out the cab
window. The lady waved and jumped,
grasped his faithful salute, while I
witnessed this fierce and thunderous
love. A tissue from her purse

caressed her eyes like a bride's veil.
Her husband's train already gone,
I noticed how well she had dressed.
The scarf about her head failed
to hide her carefully coifed hair.
She dabbed her eyes again, snapped
the Kleenex into her purse. Hope
your grandpa gets in okay, she smiled,
and left. Soon grandpa arrived,
limping toward our frozen stage,
his garlic and body odor
a gloved hand for me.

Checked Out

Mom approached the hotel desk
and asked for grandpa's room number.
The manager was sorry, but
Mr. and Mrs. Atkins had checked
out an hour ago. The problem:

Grandma was back in Omaha,
blind, obese, and drunk. She'd stopped
traveling with grandpa years ago.
My mother probably didn't notice
the intricate carving on the mahogany

desk, or smell the mix of deodorizer
and furniture polish, nor did she
appreciate the plush carpet
with the peacock design,
or the cracked leather chairs that,

no doubt, grandpa had sat in while
waiting for the "missis" to arrive
under the crystal chandelier
in the grand lobby. No, I'm sure
my mother recalled the day

she returned home from fifth grade
to discover her father had sold
her pet pig, whom she loved
so much she could never
tell me its name.

Burnt Offering

It was a nun they say invented barbed wire.
James Joyce

Sister Silvester taught me to serve
mass and diagram sentences,
but my dyslexic diagram lines
often slanted in the wrong direction.
"Your whole life sort of slants,"
she told me, and I thought she knew
my alcoholic father hadn't come home
the night my cocker spaniel died.

Soft white vestments draped,
a pristine scapula creased
precisely down the middle,
examples of her perfection
and, of course, of my ineptitude.
"You don't deserve to work God's altar,"
she said, after I forgot to serve six AM mass.
"Does Jesus forget *you?*"

Her tunic smelled soapy clean,
the scent, no doubt, of her ivory soul,
immaculate and perfectly assembled.
She was the Bride of Christ.

"If there is no God,"
she told our eighth grade class,
"it doesn't matter.
We have lived our lives
in an admirable fashion.
And if there is a God, heaven awaits,"

as it waited for my friend Bill
whom she cornered on a staircase
one cloudy September day.
"Wipe that smirk off your face,"
she demanded. He tried, but failed.
He prayed, but trapped on that stairwell

he was, evidently, out of God's range.
So Sister Sylvester pulled back
the thick folds of her purfled cuff,
and slapped him hard across his face.

And he endured that slap, though tears arose
and found their way down russet arroyos
formed the previous summer
when paint cans exploded in his
back-yard incinerator
and combusted his face.
Seven surgeries later,
Sister Sylvester conceived an angry sneer,
what those of us who loved him knew
was a bashful smile combined with fear.

Setting Up Soul, 1967

Pull the big case that contains the cymbals, snare drum, cymbal stands, and sticks out of the van. Tell the guys in the band to hold on, you're comin'. Haul in the bass drum and the floor tom. Open the bass drum case and pull out your kick beats, the ones that made the bloods smile and caused dancin' in the streets. Set up the floor tom and lean it toward the snare drum the way Marvin Gay inclines his ear to hear the grapevine. Tip the snare drum so it's ready for that rimshot— SMACK—"I feel good…!" Caress the tom-tom until you slip it onto the bass drum holder, smooth and slow, like Percy Sledge loves a woman. Set the ride cymbal on its stand and coax it down toward the floor tom, lower, a little lower, lower now—I ain't too proud to beg. Please, please, please place the crash cymbal where you can reach it fast, smash it hard, with force, super bad. Put that sock cymbal stand by me 'til it fits my left foot like a stirrup. I'll ride that mustang, Sally, all night long.

The Kansas City Soul Association

Four black singers, three white musicians,
me on drums, the Blue Bird Bar, downtown
Cheyenne, 1966—a great gig.

My 16-year-old smile
carries me home where
my mother stands in the doorway

like George Wallace at UAB.
"Did the niggers give you
a compliment?" she asks.

I hear Otis: "Try a Little
Tenderness," track my tears
into the frozen Cheyenne night,

now a seething bro to James Hood
but, unlike him, no longer seeking
admission to Mother U.

Mommy

Remember when you beat on his chest,
called him a drunken sot, pushed him
back into his old green chair,
drunk, overstuffed, his eyes crossed,
body limp and breathless?
Ward, you screamed, and
called an ambulance. Afterward
you pulled me into bed,
your hamarm vicegrip
held me against monster breasts.
Later your hamhands palmup
witnessed to the bedroom ceiling:
Please God forgive me!
I'll never say another nasty word
to him, Lord. I promise.
I was ten years old
and squirmed for release,
but you grabbed my face.
Your father almost died tonight,
you screamed, as if it was I who had
slammed his cross-eyed maybecorpse
into that chair.

Inside your carpmouth lipstick deathsmile,
your swirling bedroom purling toiletflush
melting dresser dissolving ChanelNo.5stink
deliquescing turquoise jewelry chrysallised
chemicalpink cheerylava cough medicine
vertiginous vortex of bedroom sucked
into liquefying family crapper soultrap—
not enough of me left in your hamlock,
not even enough of me left to puke.

Two days before he died,
you wished him dead.
Had the Lord heard your witness?
Had He felt your hammy palms
cup His ether? Did He

read your deathline there—
how, at ninety-six, you'd take
two days to die, husbandforgot,
sonforgot, and ask, in your deathchild
voice, *where has my mommy got to?*

Electricity's Ghost

By 1967 I still hadn't read a book,
thought history was for dead people,
math for those who didn't count,
and that there were three sexes:
men, women, and nuns.

And now, for Junior year,
the worst of the worst:
Sister Johanna would engineer English,
slap down Speech, and herd us
into Home Room where, one day,
she'd tell my friend, Paul, that he wasn't
worth the postage it would take
to send him out of the country.

All summer I listened to Dylan's
"Visions of Johanna" for guidance,
but learned only that the "ghost
of electricity howls in the bones of her face."
Maybe why Sister Johanna beamed
red when angry, like warning lights
on the missile silos that circled Cheyenne,
those heath-hidden annihilation tubes
that transformed us into targets, our futures
misshaped into crackling particles of ions.

I tried to sneak out of her classroom
on that first day, but Sister Johanna
captured me *en passant*, "I'll see *you*
after school." Her words like fallout fell.
I hadn't had time to do anything
wrong yet. What the hell?

The fragrance of Tide, her habit's scent,
dread dark as a mushroom cloud,
pulsed like a Bikini Island tsunami.
"I've got a horrible reputation," she blinked,
"And so do you. So why don't we call it even?

You give me a chance; I'll give one to you."
Her crimson face shone now more like
an airport light that beckons a landing.

A month after her proposal, I asked her
to recommend a book that I might read.
If she was about to faint, she hid it well,
and pointed to an oak case against the wall.
"That shelf belongs to me. Take any book
that strikes your fancy." Two feet of shelf,
her sole possessions on this earth
and she had offered half an inch to me.
Did she roll her eyes at my choice?
Crime and Punishment, what I hoped
might be a detective story.

She cried when I told her, years later,
that she had launched me that day.
She'd pushed a button that freed me
from my hiding place in a lonely silo
along the prairie. An ignition
that led not only to war,
but to *War and Peace*,
A Separate Peace,
A Farewell to Arms.

Bank of America

I stretch my finger across the room
and reel it in again, a psychedelic fisherman
tripping the Campus Shop, Laramie, Wyoming, 1969.
In limps Lagerkvist's Dwarf in the form
of my crippled "friend" Gil. "You know what
those fuckin' hippies have done?" The psilocybin
I'd ingested Picassoed his face. I hear his voice,
but can't find his mouth. "They burned
down the fuckin' Bank of America!" I'd never
heard of the Bank of America. I thought
it must be THE bank where they kept ALL the money—
every gazillion dollar bill—made in America.

Ten days later my draft board declares
my objection conscientious. I drink half a fifth
of scotch and drive to San Francisco to look
for alternative service, but really to find Suzi,
my untouchable Catholic high school sweetie
turned hippie at UC Santa Barbara. I find her
in a student hovel in Isla Vista. We walk
hand in hand on the campus. Her long brown hair
caresses her face, snug white jeans and sleeveless
blouse promise my bellbottomed, sandaled self
the free love I'd heard about.

"What's that?" I ask as we approach a huge mound
of rubble. "The Bank of America," she says. "We
burned it down a week ago." "No shit," I say
and fend off the inevitable Gil hippie-hater
flashback. A bearded man sits atop the rubble,
chants, plays harmonium. "Who's that?" I ask.
"Allen Ginsberg," she says. We don't stop to listen
because, at 19, I'd decided he wasn't a good poet.

Suzi waltzes me to the beach where the wind
sculpts her breasts tight against her top, her
hair wild in the breeze. We find a loge for love
in the sand, her breath sweet across tongue

and lips. Something wet weeps through my pants,
something gushy and foreign. I grab my butt;
my fingers turn black and sticky. Tar coats my ass
like the darkest road of the great American nightmare.
We watch the gooey lumps ride the greasy waves
from one of our first, and worst, oil spills, and sigh
as this moment turns to rubble and dies.

Shave

I pulled the curtains around his bed
and helped him off with his pants

The smell was horrible

I went through his pockets
all he had was a subway token from New York City
and a filthy comb   Something odd

the teeth of the comb were moving
We both had to shower   not together of course

with Quell soap   the only soap that
killed the lice and the eggs   that moved
across the comb

Then I shaved him

his grey stubble   ragged
I lathered him up   went to work

His neck looked like cured leather

He talked nonstop about everything
that came to his mind
I tried to follow   his words a salad I could not eat

I think he enjoyed our closeness
I think he liked the warm water and soap suds

But what of that NYC subway token

> I'd never been to New York
> I was nineteen
> a conscientious objector working the ancient open wards
> of Denver General Hospital in 1969

Had he been to NYC   Had he travelled by train to Denver

sunk in the doldrums of Larimer Street

He had been someone's child

II. Wild Pitch

You must have chaos within you
to give birth to a dancing star.
—Friedrich Nietzsche, *Thus Spoke Zarathustra*

They Are Not Long

To Ernest Dowson

The tiny wasp
that's been bothering
me all morning
wallops down
a half-empty glass
of orange juice
(or is it half-full)
which I set out
to lure him from
his yearning over
my morning repast.

He could have wallowed
in a riot of roses
laughed his way
through his day,
but chose to provoke
my hate, my love
of bait.

So leisurely led
to his sticky demise
in orange patina
where he flails,
weeps to free himself.
How simple to lure,
whether louche or not,
a being besotted
with desire, whose sting,
disguised as need,
drowns in life's mire.

Three Blatherskites and You're Out

...I've got to get my bread and butter back. That slider is what I am.
—Charlie Morton, baseball pitcher

So many struggle all their
                lives
to find themselves;
create and sustain
                an identity.

Psychoanalysts have written
about it ad nauseam:
                Everyone
from Erik Erikson who
alleged
to know just when you
acquired one, supplied
charts and nifty slogans
                for proof,

to Stolorow and the relational
                crowd
who claimed we
chameleons
were who we were depending
on whomever we were with,

to a French blatherskite
who would flatulate
in restaurants to get
                attention.
I'm talking about Jacques
Lacan who claimed

that your ego
(an amalgam of bad
                snapshots
of someone else),

can never know

        your subject,

and that this entire

        situation

enrages us forever.

But then these guys
never met Charlie Morton,
never watched him

        open

on the mound for the

        Pittsburgh Pirates—

never had to face his
ferocious slider,
or eat his bread and butter.

Furry Bee Motel

Outside cars zig or zag, or not, snow everywhere, while Marianne, our infant son's
Hungarian nanny, calls every relative she has,
even those who only speak Hungarian.
"For God's sake," she pleads, "stay off the roads

in the snow!" Her plea is made in English,
she having only a few Hungarian words
(she tells our son to brush his *zupies,*
but that's Polish). Who knows what
her Hungarian relatives think she's saying:
Don't piss on the pierogies? Hide the cabbage
from grandma? Between calls Marianne paces,

chain-smokes in our living room, and balances
beneath her Marge Simpson beehive hairdo
packed with the essentials: envelopes, stamps, pencils,
pens, a carton of Camel Lites, Tampax, compacts,
sandwich bags, lipstick, Chapstick, and paper clips.
You think I'm joking. You think this junk couldn't hide
in one woman's head. But I'm not joking. This stuff
and more is trapped within the tight faux-blond
folds of Marianne's hair. What of the Geritol,

and spaceships in there, the nitwits, complexes,
neuroses, spring roses, the pink and blue geraniums,
even (I know this is hard to believe) Geronimo's thumb
and index finger from his right (tomahawk) hand?
You could get Shakespearian about a wench like this,
for trapped atop her dome-skillet is a brass band,
a marriage band, and a list of banned movies

provided by the Legion of Decency in 1964. How,
you might ask, does she maintain an upright posture?
Ask an authority on black holes, someone like Stephen
Hawking. All I know is that within her spun folds
of gold there are the Stations of the Cross,
three hundred holy cards attesting that she is,

essentially, a good girl, the nuns' pet, the pet
project of a bleeding Jesus and his Holy Mother.
You're thinking, this is disgusting; this isn't poetry,
people are laughing. You wish I'd get serious. Okay,
here's what isn't located in Marianne's hair, but is
in her hair nevertheless: a daughter who broke her
heart when she eloped; another daughter whom she
can't control; and her husband, John, to whom she
sweetly reads the newspaper every day because
he is illiterate. These are the *zupies* that gnaw her soul
and brux her being from sun to moon to sun again.
Thank God, you're thinking, he got off his hilarity horse

and back to what poetry is all about: MISERY.
You're out of luck. There's more aboard the furry bee
motel above Marianne's brain: any intelligent cootie
or dandruff-chip could find, lodged within her
curls, the relics of three barn animals who attended
the birth of Christ, thread from the Shroud of Turin,
all fifteen decades of the rosary, a pre-Vatican II
Catholic Missal circa 1957, a bottle of holy water

from Lourdes, a pair of chattering teeth, a gismo that,
when concealed in her palm, buzzes when she shakes
someone's hand, causing minutes of uproarious laughter.
Snug within her finely spun pelt hangs a bona-fide
"Life of the Party" certificate from the Dick Cheney
Academy of Reality Obliteration, a newspaper article
describing the incarceration of Cowboy Bob for child

molestation in the sixties, a vial purporting to contain
half a cc of Pee Wee Herman's gusher that got him
arrested and ruined his career, and an air pocket
of irony. Everything she needs except instructions
on how to keep those she loves safe
when they drive in the snow.

Wild Pitch

You've never seen a ball game
'til you've heard one on the radio.
Tonight, the Tigers come back,
down 4-0, score four in the seventh,
the fourth on a wild pitch.
The wildness is up to you:
the ball hit the catcher in his nads
causing him to puke and lose the orb
under mounds of chili dog and granola?
Or the ball rolls off the catcher's glove
slamming the umpire's mask so hard
he thinks he's attending Mass,
transubstantiation only seconds away.
He hears altar bells and is perplexed:
they don't use bells at Mass anymore.
Or the ball turns into a Great Horned Owl
who flies over the big-wig section
behind home plate and snatches Earl,
some rich lady's affenpinscher, faster
than you can say "brand new ballgame."
The rich lady eats right, jogs, has a trainer,
and then something like this happens,
out of left field, except it was out
of the pitchers' mound. No matter
how it happened, the Tiger runner scores
from third, the Kansas City pitcher is removed,
and a rich lady calls the affenpinscher hot line
where she's told there are plenty Earls
where that one came from.

The Game

Twenty-one years of Ariel beam
from under a baseball cap. "We're going
to the game tonight," he says,
"The Portland Beavers vs. The Tacoma Rainiers."
He knows that I'll love it
and apologizes to his mother
who thinks baseball should last
as long as it takes to eat a foot-long and fries.
Five dollars a piece that night to sit
behind home plate. It turns out that
the difference between triple A baseball
and the major leagues is 25 bucks a seat.
The scoreboard is hand operated:
no hits, no runs, and a bald head
where the errors should be.
It's hair cut night! Ten barbers
stationed in PGE Park give fans
their choice of haircuts. A radio
announcer sits in the 20th row,
swinging his arms over his head,
doing a Harry Caray imitation
during the 7th inning stretch.
Arms around each other Ari and I sing,
"Take me out to the ball game."
"I love you, dad," he says.
I kiss his cheek, laugh out loud,
slap him on the back. I really
don't care if I ever get back.

Elvis Presley Patch

Let's face it,
there is no hair left
on top of my head.
Even if I bought a designer mop,
or had a hair transplant
and looked like I'd head-butted
a porcupine whose quills
injected fake hair follicles
into my scalp,
the hair that my mother
and father put on my head
is gone forever.

It's taken thirty years
for me to lose my hair.
When Ariel was little
its gradual loss alarmed him.
He'd grab a maculate clump
close to my forehead—
my Elvis Presley patch, he called it—
and tug. Why couldn't it spread
to the bald spots, he wanted to know.
You can have some of my hair, Daddy,
he offered, not yet bound to ratiocination.
I'd thank him, then tickle and hold him
down until he said, *Forgiveness*
Holy Father Papal Emissary,
a fallen Catholic's rendition
of *Say Uncle.*

I write this to my friend Sharon
whose hair has just fallen out
in the shower—all at once.
She thought, maybe, it wouldn't happen
to her, but it did. As usual
she's positive: *It means*
I've got powerful drugs
fighting the cancer, she tells me.

I bet you look like a cute
little Buddha nun, I write,
and fail to mention the flood of fate
that shines like a nimbus
in both our eyes.

Catching Jesus

"Ohhhhhh Jeeeeesus," I'd yell,
and Zorba would redefine desire,
reconfigure yearning, reconceptualize predation,
and lose it in the way only a 95-pound
white German Shepherd who thought
that Jesus was a squirrel could.
After "sit," "come," "stay," and "down,"
I'd taught him that the true vicar of Christ
on this earth was a squirrel.

Interrupting his wails and squeals at the door,
his psalms of religious fervor, I'd imitate
a southern Baptist preacher. "Do you believe?"
I'd ask. "Do you accept Jesus as your personal savior?"
"Yes!" he'd bark, "Hallelujah," he'd cry.
When his zeal reached launch-strength
I'd let fly the door. He'd scream down our porch
like a Comanche in those old racist westerns,
or like fat Auntie Ursal when she caught me
spying on her flesh-folds during her bath.

Imagine a young stunned squirrel
as this white toothy blur blasts
across the yard; a vision of massive jaws
closing on its soft, crunchable, body.
Imagine the shrill realization
of being food. Even before terror,
the squirrel brain transmits *scram*,
guides it to the nearest tree
where safety hides in tall branches.

Its parents, who know this game,
wait until the last second,
then bolt up a sycamore
leaving Zorba to dance,
a squealing sparring partner,
roping-a-dope for Jesus.
He'd stand guard, like a soldier

on Mount Olivet waiting to drive
his sword home, although the Z man
would never vinegar a wound.

At night, when raccoons and skunks
made it too dangerous to let him
run untethered into our yard,
I might yell "Oh Jesus" anyway,
to test the verisimilitude of his faith.
The Zorbster would run panicked circles
round our living room, screaming
and moaning, dog language for,
there must be some way out of this house
without relying on these human nitwits
to open a door. Clearly he was hoping
for a miracle, the parting of the walls,
the dissolving of the windows, or visions
of many Jesuses dashing around the house,
on top of the bed, under the bed, in the bathroom,
caught in the sink, ready to sacrifice themselves
on the altar of his ferocious delight.
But there were no miracles for Zorba,
whose happiest moments were
with us, wherever we were.

Last week his great legs finally failed.
His decline was swift. He still sought Jesus,
but a viewing reduced him to a mournful howl,
front paws painfully raising his kingly chest,
then back down. He could do no more.

His execution was scheduled
for 3:30 in the afternoon.
At 9 that morning he made it
20 feet down our walkway.
"We can't do this today," I told my wife
who, always more connected to reality,
shook her head.

At noon he soiled himself in our front yard,

his sphincters deadened by his diseased spine.
His desire to please puddled in shame,
he turned away from us, the lake, and life.
I held him when the doctor started the injection.
He took it sitting up, too regal to lie down.
I told him how much I loved him,
and what a good dog he had been.
He'd catch Jesus now, I said.

I told him this and patted his soft white fur
until he no longer felt my desperate touch.

False Dawn

He flashed, refulgent,
on vision's periphery
almost three feet high,
green feathers and greatness.

I was walking Mugsi
when I glimpsed
the wild turkey hobbling
up a neighbor's drive.

His right leg injured, held high,
he hopped forward, resolute,
toward his certain demise. I
wondered what would get him—

a dog probably, maybe a hawk.
What got me was how he kept moving,
carrying himself with such verdant dignity.
The next day I wait for my wife

at the rehab. A black man inches
his way into the waiting room.
Worn sweatpants gray as dawn,
he uses two canes to move

his stiff and aimless legs.
Each step an infinity that
reminds me of the theory
in quantum physics that

the closer you get to a star
the farther it moves away.
"How are you, young man?"
he asks me, although

we are two oldsters close
in age. "Fine thanks,"
I say, and ask him how he is.

"I'm elegant," he smiles. "I'm elegant."

Flash Cards

Someone's gonna be in trouble.

Some kid's Spanish flash cards
strewn along Maple Avenue
blown down the sidewalk,
lodged in ivy ground cover,
stuck under decrepit concrete
of disintegrating sidewalk
like a schoolboy's T-shirt caught
in the grasp of a detention teacher.

¿Como se escribe, *big fuck up*, en espanol?[2]

How did they get there?

Blown haphazardly out of
an errant backpack pocket?
Thrown out a bus window
by the fat older kid? A new torture
for the quiet one with glasses?
(Will he explode a dirty bomb
in a football stadium
when he grows up?)

¿Puedo usar el sacapuntas?[3]

Or a petulant toss and a curse—

who needs this shit?
Studying Spanish is un-American.
Mexicans are un-American.

Preguntale a otro estudiante.[4]

They're everywhere: Major League Baseball,
sitcoms, movies, rock bands,
doctors, lawyers, writers
and restaurant owners.

Even the ATM offers a Spanish option.
Maybe gray Governor
Jan Brewer, supercharged
from her victory in Arizona,
relaxing in Pittsburgh,
where there are few Latinos,
grabbed those flash cards and
threw them across Maple Avenue.

Not in my America,
she might have yelled.
We want our country back!
Give us our country back!

¡Cierra los libros![5]

Sartre and Simone Get Married

We are gathered here today
in the eyes of the Others,
to join together in subjugation
these two beings-in-the-world

who stand before us as subject
and subject, each a sink hole that sucks
in the other, like water swirling down
the drain after a bath is done.

These two fleshy beings have overcome
their nausea so as to endure this ceremony.
Repeat after me: *I, Jean-Paul,*

pledge my love to Ms. de Beauvoir,
primarily as a ruse to trick her into
not stealing my freedom. May you
transcend my ego forever.

I, Simone, accept your look,
the gaze that objectifies me because,
having allowed you to steal my freedom
by loving me, I have infuriated millions

of women across the world who never
thought I'd abide such an abomination.
They're (h)omelet eaters, second sexers,
and they've got plans for you, pal.

And so, in the name of Husserl, Heidegger,
and Merleau-Ponty, I pronounce you
subject and object, master and slave,

For Itself and In Itself, for eternity.
What *mauvaise foi* has put together,
let authenticity never pull asunder.

You may kiss the flesh of the other.
Congratulations and repeat after me:
Hell, it is the other.

In Memory of Frederick August Kittel, Jr.

His mother worried, wanted
only the best for him.
Sent him to Catholic school.
Every morning at St. Steven's, a note
on his desk: "Go home, Nigger." Mourning reborn
as an ashen Phoenix—impossible to kill.
A picture of his ninth grade class at Central Catholic
shows Freddie, the only African American,
his head turned to the side—bowed,
as if by a hangman's noose.

In this ocean of white,
he was Pittsburgh's black gem,
its king, the train we loved to ride;
our eighth guitar, our shining man.

Spit out by Central Catholic, he landed
in Gladstone High School, across the street from home.
He joined the college club, tried to impress
his teacher with a twenty-page paper on Napoleon.
The teacher, a black man, refused to believe
he had written it. Freddie threw Napoleon into the trash
and gave us Caesar—but that was later.
He told people he never returned to school,
but he shot baskets outside the principal's window
for days, hoping someone would tell him
to come back. No one did.

In this ocean of white,
he was Pittsburgh's black gem,
its king, the train we loved to ride;
our eighth guitar, our shining man.

August found the Carnegie Library in Oakland,
a jump shot from Central Catholic.
He thought it contained every book ever written,
and he tried to read them all.
Soon before he died, the State of Pennsylvania

passed a law that allowed Carnegie Library
to issue August a high school diploma.
At the ceremony he thanked everyone—
then complained about the savage inequalities
killing hope, snuffing the spirit, stifling
kids like him who loved knowledge,
but were judged the wrong color.

In this ocean of white,
he was Pittsburgh's black gem,
its king, the train we loved to ride;
our eighth guitar, our shining man.

Despite ten plays, a wave of awards,
cancer came after August Wilson
with a catholic viciousness.
He didn't let it destroy his soul.
"I've been blessed," he said, "I'm ready,"
dying to this life at sixty.

In this ocean of white,
he was Pittsburgh's black gem,
its king, the train we loved to ride;
our eighth guitar, our shining man.

Michigan Icebreaker

So there he stands,
old Frank on the ice, naked,
his face a broken mask
of glee, raising his ax
and bringing it down
on the frozen surface
with the force of a man
in his twenties. The metallic

ring of ax on ice
echoes over the lake
like a rustic violin
causing neighbors to rustle
last night's ashes
and bring their embers
aglow—nature's neon lights bright
along this vast circumference.

We all know he's crazy
and love him for it.
Eighty-six years of Frank
in fighting shape, someone
to whom a nice widow lady
would serve eggs
from her finest designer chickens
and wouldn't turn down
should he ask for a blanket
and a body to warm his
cold and muscled mass.

Fall, Up North

Everything dying up here
is so alive. We walk
through a maple leaf blast,
the deep red explosion
coating us in color, anointing

our entry into gamboge
birch and aspen—
leaves lit as if from within.
No wonder our dog, Mugsi,
thinks they're as energized

and happy as her tail.
Our neighbor, Jim, on
this morning walk with us,
points to a patch of myrtle
he's planted that will creep,
if we live long enough,
towards our property.
Judy sits on a step

at the public access park,
and for the trillionth time
is flummoxed by the sun
beads bouncing across
Walloon Lake, its blue
liquid canvas conducting
a daytime lightshow.

On the way back Judy
wants to turn right when
I know we should turn
left. Jim knows it, too,
and we watch as Judy
finally reads the road sign,
sighs, and says we should turn
left. Never undone, she declares
that Jim is right while I am wrong

(that's forty years of marriage
in a song). Hungry,
at walk's end, we decide on lunch
at the Odawa Casino. They
once owned all we just saw:
their leaves a bed for spring trillium,
their eyes the hues of autumn
identical to the land we love. Now

their ears the mind-numbing
clang of slot machines, their eyes
every color *not* known to nature.
We get the senior buffet special,
all you can eat for seven bucks apiece.
They've done a fine job with the casino,
the food is spectacular, Judy and Jim
eat the fish while I enjoy a steaming
bowl of bean and ham soup. Mugsi

waits asleep in the car. She dreams
of leaves that fly away from her
like the moths and butterflies
she loves to chase. I dream
that we four will take this walk
again, this flashcut out of chaos,
this path of right turns.

The Sounds of Wet Grass Sobbing

I heard sounds of wet grass.
—Rachel Jeantel[6]

Of course she heard the sounds
of wet grass. She heard the soggy sobs
of a failed world, the weeping ghosts
of Emmett Till, Medgar Evers,
and Martin Luther King, Jr. She heard

the lugubrious wails of our gun culture's
cry for help and its explosive, murderous
response. She heard four hundred years
of Nothing Changes, of hope fettered
in society's sedges. She saw Jim Crow,

rapacious and reborn, take wing
and hasp her soul to the raised eye-
brows and pompous voices
of rubicund, toothy, television
commentators who pitied her

poor education and homespun manner.
What would those omniscients have said
of Tomas Tranströmer's, "stars stomping
in their stalls,"[7] or that wizened old man who
heard America bluff in those grassleaves?

The Great Tactician

There you were naked
        at the river's edge,
                exhausted
                        after your two-day swim.
Nausicaa stood over you

when you awoke
        a smile of yearning
                and compassion
                        on her soft lips.
You thought she was

beautiful and terrifying.
        You didn't know whether
                to grab her knees
                        and hope for mercy,
or use your honeyed speech,

beg some clothes,
        the direction into town.
                You chose words and
                        she showed you a mercy
                                that, had you paid attention,
could have changed western civilization.

                            Instead

you ate her father's food,
        tossed the discus around,
                impressed her brother
                  and all the boys,
                        but once back in Ithaca,
you destroyed your enemies

with a wrath that would have shamed Achilles.
        Your boy even hung their lovers,
                watched, with glee,
their tiny feet dance to death.

What of *their* pleas for mercy,
      Great Gamelegs?
          What of Nausicaa's compassion,
             man of all occasions?
You chose words and so did they,

but your heart was cold with greatness.
      We could have had
          three thousand years of mercy.

               Instead

your savagery endures:
          the glory of dead heroes

             piled one
             atop
             another
             and
             another.

Time After Time

Husserl and Heidegger had their problems
especially after Marty became a Nazi
and threw Eddie, his Jewish mentor,
out of Freiburg University, but one thing
upon which they agreed: Clock Time
was a scientistic ruse used to seduce us
into believing in priests in white coats,
their statistics and control groups.
It was Lived Time, they said, that counted
(so to say), and it's true that five minutes
spent in line for an ice cream differs wildly
from five minutes on execution day.
Still, imagine the old Nazi's embarrassment
when Clock Time hopped on his bed and said,
"So long, Marty, you're dead." Or perhaps
there's a lost notebook entry written
in his awful German: "Proximally
and for the most part, but really
exactly and regrettably, Dasein is
that being whose very Being ends
when Clock Time declares it has."

Walking Townsend Road, Petoskey, Michigan

One day it's the red-twigged dogwoods
ringed by ragweed yellows and
chicory blues that clarify mind
and confirm insignificance.

Another day it's the garter snake
whose crushed head reassures
and saddens, the long green body
pocked with purple checks
stretched out on the southbound lane,
the sheen of life still coats its skin,
its breath, now, of the expired world
where there is only awe.

Today, like Buddhas at sunset,
three sandhill cranes stand
on Billeau's farm facing West,
enacting contrariness. Rusty
feathers hug their shoulders
like prayer robes,
as maples and ashes
ablaze in crimson and orange,
conduct cornstalk symphonies
in the dying autumn sun.

Against sunset's gleam
it's hard to tell, at first,
whether those cranes are deer
or birds or monks.
Their hunched silhouettes mark
the force of sun over meadow,
breeze over grass: a tyranny of calm
in this bloody, battle-fed world.

Positive Babinski

What tickles a newborn
devastates when old.
It could be Lou Gehrig's Disease,
Multiple Sclerosis, Muscular Dystrophy,
a stroke of very bad luck.
How could something positive
be so negative?

This nerve-thin thread
will snap one day;
we know that,
but don't believe it,
the breaking point uncertain.

There is no treatment
and yet there may be
one to balance benefits
against side effects:

a prosthetic soul
replacement that causes
a caustic limp, a hitch,
a slant, that makes a person
twist in circles
until the end.

His Voice

For Phil Druker

Tea warms my throat
brings belonging   grounding
the sense of home—

but does Phil, dying
of cancer, feel this?
Does a man loosed
by morphine
know or care
about the pleasures
of home? Or is he

leaving home   waiting
to abandon that alluvial
gobbet called "I,"
that rickety shack of self
once strong and stark
now disappearing
like the shimmer
from a highway baking
in the sun?

The countdown   the march
beating drum   down
of a ticking clock   thread
that leaves the spool bare.

We hadn't spoken for forty years.
Now his voice isn't
his own, but a timbre
of unimaginable suffering:
the sonorous dissonance
of anti-nausea meds—
no longer his voice,
but *that* voice.

Grammar of Change

First, like a hit-squad,
they liquidated the intimate
second person. We don't say
"thou" or "thee" anymore. Even
the Quakers have let it go. Still,
how I yearn to say to my beloved,
"Thou art my strength, my Buddha
light," without her thinking

I'd been drinking too much Bud Lite.
Then they killed the Oxford comma
that comes before "and"
in a series of three as in,
"When my alliteration gave out,
I floundered, fell, and failed." Now

my friend Jim says that in ten years
we won't use semicolons anymore,
as if we won't need to combine one
independent clause with another or
provide a substitute for those tired old
conjunctions. Well they can have
my semicolons when they pry them
out of my cold, crashed, word processor.

But then, who am I kidding?
Long ago, in his classic bout
with Parmenides, Heraclitus
landed a cosmic K.O.
Our condition is change,
whose main clause, death,
is all we really have,
everything we fear the most;
all that punctuates our lives.

Confucius

He was a small man
and very old,
old even at birth.
He had so many wise sayings,
but he never cautioned
to look both ways before crossing,
or not to trust everyone
you meet, or believe
everything you read.
He never taught a child
to keep his hands off a flaming burner,
or not to stare at someone
who was crying,
or not to ask a waitress
to bring a glass of water
after she brought the juice you ordered
after she brought the side
of blue cheese
for your wings
after she took back
the ranch dressing that came
with the wings
after you changed your order to
wings from stuffed mushrooms
after you cancelled the surf and turf
to order the Dover sole without capers
in the white wine sauce.
And he never said,
"Baseball wrong: Man
with four balls cannot walk."

But he did say,
"Wherever you go,
go with all your heart."
And he said,
"Our greatest glory is not
in never falling,
but in rising every time

we fall."

Robin Williams, as Armand,
told his gay lover Albert
(Nathan Lane) in *The Birdcage*
that he'd have to buy a grave plot
next to Albert's so
he'd never miss the laughs.
That was Armand's way
of talking Albert out of
killing himself.

I wonder where Robin Williams
is buried.

Confucius said, "The funniest people
are the saddest once."

Being and Nothingness and Being

Thus it amounts to the same thing
whether one gets drunk alone
or is a leader of nations.
—J.P. Sartre

We crossed the Arno
at a tremendous clip
to the Uffizi where
we stood in darkness
in the courtyard
and listened to a man
play electric violin
to Albinoni's Adagio.
It would have been sacrilegious
to move, so we stood still,
our silence,
our immobility,
his cornerstone,
and the worlds.'

*

All these years
Sartre was right.
Consciousness *is*
that nothingness
spread in between me
and what I perceive.
The clearer the nothingness,
the more crystalline
the world—
why Laramie
was so appealing:
so much nothingness,
a real abundance!
Now the Higgs boson
fills our world—
that nothing

that makes something
exist between me
and everything else.
The world's a shadow box
filled with cosmological Jell-O.

*

Your breath steam
visible in the cold
Wyoming dawn,
the heat from
his flank
your only warmth.
You held the oat cake
flat on your hand,
let Baldy's muzzle
quiver it off your palm.
The sound of his chewing
made you hungry
amid the dust motes
and hay. His crunch
crunch crunch
regular,
rhythmic,
the calm timepiece
of the barn.

III. Milliseconds of Mystery

*Snatching the eternal out of the desperately fleeting
is the great magic trick of human existence.*
  —Tennessee Williams

.

Half the Distance

Someday we'll measure it all:
the number of feet to friendship,
inches to night, centimeters to soul,
miles to memory, bits to bathos;
how much RAM for romance. Life

will be so much easier. Truth,
a keystroke click; morality
on our monitors. Calculators
will compute the lengths of love,
reduce ambiguity to nanoseconds,

and prove Zeno's paradox.
How *could* anything move
in such a world? But
then there's your face,
my love, dream-eyes, infinity-

lips, cheeks of charity.
Your smile shames calculus
to folly. Milliseconds of mystery,
counted, divided, and squared,
can't capture your eyes.

Rach II

For Judy

His lips travel this music
along her silky skin fragrance
toward her dawn, eye mirror,
his hand hovers hope, musk
hair, the most gracious sin
of tongue, taut temptation. His
fingers sing her mouth, trace

its curve, swim watermelon
breath. This music springs, fall
leaves tremble the meadowland,
snow hides, eager, just behind
Tantalus' breeze—Tantalus whose
desire made Death wait and wait
and wait while he reached toward

what yearned and languished
the barely reachable, chaosed
in love's love, life's promise –
the must-be-broken; but who
reached toward the one
who reached back, she
who held time, hymned

eternity across a frozen lake,
smiled his soul. He chanted,
no matter how long it lasts,
it's not long enough, to her
who made his world glow
warm for his time,
the only time he had.

On Wealthy St. in Grand Rapids

I look at a window
that isn't anymore, a plank
of sun-bleached plywood
where the pane should be;
the weatherboard, splintered,
worn by days of snow and sun,
survives long after the sill's decay.
Judy couldn't make

this trip; pain weathers her body,
arthritis in every joint—Crohn's Disease.
Thirty years ago her surgeon
drew a circle three inches west
and two inches south of her belly
button—the spot where he'd construct
her cherry tomato stoma.
Every day of her life she
attaches her ileostomy bag
after cutting out the flange
and carving flesh-colored glowworm
strands of silky paste placed
so to affix the pouch
to her tummy. Sometimes Judy

and I dance naked and wild
around our bedroom. I say,
I love you in your birthday suit. Judy
says, My birthday suit plus one,
worried that I don't love that extra part
clothed with a red flowered flannel
cover, like one of her nighties.

Asparagus

Remember how we had that terrific view
        of Cheesman Park
from the third floor of your apartment
        in Denver?
I'd never imagined living so grandly.

Your large living room with its plush green
        carpet. Your tiny
kitchen where you cooked that first
        dinner for me.
Remember? You had asked whether there

were any foods I didn't like. I forgot
        to mention asparagus.
If my mother made asparagus I couldn't
        eat anything
she cooked in her kitchen.

And for that first dinner you cooked
        asparagus in lemon
sauce. When I told you I couldn't eat it
        you sat next to me,
your long dark hair an ocean of Eros,

your eyes hazel torches that burned
        through my past;
your breath sweet with lemon zest.
        Give it a try,
you said. I did, and it tasted like

a universe about to begin. It's still
        my favorite vegetable.
And then there was your bedroom,
        the huge bed
we were unable to leave that Saturday

we were supposed to drive to Estes Park.
        We meant to,

but we kept making love, getting dressed,
      and making more love
until the day slipped down the tongue

of the Milky Way. Forty years later,
      we try to pay bills,
but we don't make it because we get up
      too late and eat
lunch right after breakfast and must go

to the grocery store where we'll buy a roast
      to serve
when our son and daughter-in-law arrive
      for Christmas.
The difference now? All our moments

make love. Our eyes, our words, float
      on the slow tip
of time—and we know years—we two
      thickandthinners,
hurtling towards the inevitable blur of us.

Just Once

After losing the big game,
I'd like to hear a star athlete say,
You know why we lost? We lost
because Bruno is porking coach's wife
and Jesus is not just smiting him,
He's smiting our entire team;

or some centenarian attribute his longevity
to ardent atheism:
my long life was possible
because guilt never sat on my eyelids
like the coins of the dead.
I never worried that I'd burn

in a metaphysical furnace
run by a dork with a pitchfork;
never fretted about sitting on an old
bearded guy's right or left hand,
or, god forbid, one of his knees.

The downside? I can't hope
to see again those I so dearly loved
in this life. We'll never talk

about what we missed.
I'll never hold my wife again,
stroke her silky hair, or feel
her breath upon my cheek.

Still, we die wrapped in the loves
we were lucky enough to garner
in this life. Whatever those last minutes
I'll be grateful for my time
on this green orb. I'd gladly do it again
and again. Who knows, maybe
Nietzsche got that part right.

The Between World

Afternoon sun lit the green hues
of the cactus behind my analyst chair—
the cactus with an obscene curve lustily
lambasted, one awful session, by a buxom patient
as a cockroach crawled across her chest.
It took months for us to work through
my phallic cactus and that nasty trope
between her breasts. Still, sunlight always
returned calm, reestablished peace,
but nothing surpassed the transcendent power
of the train whistle that sounded every day
between 2:30 and 3PM. One patient, a woman
with multiple marital transgressions,
always stopped to admire that haunting sound,
even while describing incest as an adult
with her older brother—putting me into
a mute place that made that whistle
a lifelong soother. The sound, I understand,
from some obscure Tibetan text, I'll hear
as I start my journey, after breath,
toward the Between World.

My Religion

For Robert Fanning

What to do with those tiny souls in Limbo
now that Limbo is no more?
Do they join the gluttonous shades in Purgatory
who ate meat on Fridays?

Maybe St. Christopher will carry the Limbos
and the latter day carnivores
across the River Styx and back to ...
Whoops! They did away with St. Christopher, too.
He's not in the moving business anymore.

Jesus perched an eagle on my neighbor's mailbox
in answer to her prayer:
should she buy a condo on the lake, another home?
The sale complete,
the market crashed like a featherless eagle drone.
A broker's license was, evidently,
something Jesus didn't own.

Jesus never talks to me, and I feel lucky.
The people I know who hear from Jesus
have had that doctor's visit we all dread,
or arrived home to find a spouse in bed
with their best worst friend,
or better yet, dead.

My religion is the umber
exposed ambiguity of grass,
autumn's redefinition of light;
the birch tree that sways
amid sweet leafmeal smells,
framed by roiling lake waves which reform dirt:
the diet of a limber god who mocks
my somber moods and chainsaws my hang-ups.

Timber!

Born Again

You want to be born again?
I'll give you born again: live,

savor each breath,
inhales and exhales,

the blossom of tomatoes and oregano
exploding in your frying pan,

the smell of garlic and olive oil,
the grand bouquet of basil,

your lover's eye-sparkle,
her lilting voice, Pavarotti's tenor,

Jim Harrison's novels—
everything that makes it so hard

to leave our troubled planet.
Stay near to those with whom you

shared your brindled years: comfort
them, stroke their dying hair, smell

their fragrant mortality. They
walked with you along this path,

this path that appears then disappears
like a sleigh inside a blizzard.

Vows

After Marc Chagall's "The Birthday Kiss"

He: I promise to carry a backpack all over Europe on our vacation even though it has nothing in it but your stuff.

She: I promise to go to three baseball games a season and not force you to leave after the seventh inning.

He: I promise to pick up my underwear and put it in the hamper even though I have to walk an extra foot to do so.

She: I promise to go to one disaster flick a year even if it costs me a nightmare.

He: I promise to wait patiently while you primp in the bathroom, making us half-an-hour late for a party we've know about for months.

She: I promise to ask politely, instead of angrily, that you take a shower after you've played drums for three days straight and want to have sex with me.

He: I promise to wait with you while your dinner heats in the microwave even though my dinner is ready and the news is on in the living room.

She: I promise to pretend that I didn't see you pick your nose and flick the results onto our living room carpet.

He: I promise to change the toilet tissue roll every time it runs out in my presence —or at least most of the time.

She: I promise not to threaten divorce when you cut your fingernails and leave the clippings in your dessert bowl.

He: I promise to let you get a word in edgewise.

She: I promise to laugh at your jokes even though I've heard them a hundred times and never thought they were funny in the first place.

He: I promise to stop criticizing you for mumbling when I know that I've lost forty percent of the hearing in my left ear.

She: I promise to love you forever.

He: I promise to love you more than that.

He and She: I promise to hold you on that last night and float with you above the world and disappear into that land the fools call death.

1 Words carved on Charles Bukowski's gravestone.
2 How do you write…in Spanish?
3 Can I use the pencil sharpener?
4 Call on another student.
5 Close your books!
6 Rachel Jeantel testifying at the George Zimmerman murder trial.
7 Tomas Tranströmer, "Autumnal Archipelago," in *The Deleted World*, Trans. R. Robertson, (New York: Farrar, Straus and Giroux, 2006), 3.

Acknowledgements

Atlanta Review: "Half the Distance"
Avalon Literary Review: "False Dawn"
Barbaric Yawp: "The Game"
The Bear River Review: "The Sound of Wet Grass Sobbing," "Walking Townsend Road, Petoskey, Michigan," "Fall, Up North," "Setting Up Soul—1968," "So Important," "Time After Time," "The Between World"
The Front Weekly: "Vows"
Icon: Magazine for Literature and Art: "Born Again," "Jesus's Mother Didn't Have Blond Hair"
Jerry Jazz Musician: "Flash Cards"
Literary Life Chap Book (Poetry Anthology), Vol. 4: "Goodbye" (3rd place—Literary Life Poetry contest, 2012)
The Paterson Literary Review: "What She Held—1966" (Editor's Choice—2013 Allen Ginsberg Poetry Award), "Burnt Offering," "My Religion," "My First Poetry Teacher"
The Pittsburgh Post-Gazette: "Rach II," "In Memory of Frederick August Kittel, Jr."
The Potomac: A Journal of Poetry and Politics: "Include a Brief Biographical Statement (Three Lines) with Your Poetry Submission"
The Quotable: "Michigan Icebreaker" (reprinted in *Baily's Beads*)
Shadow Road Quarterly: "Grammar of Change"
Spitball: "Wild Pitch"
VerseWrights: "Marmalade," "Daydream," "Shave," "Elvis Presley Patch," "On Wealthy St. In Grand Rapids," "Catching Jesus," "His Voice," "The Great Tactician"
Wild Violet Magazine: "Electricity's Ghost"
Xanadu: "The Furry Bee Motel" (as "Marianne")
Z-Composition: "At Ten I Thought Everyone Had A Shoebox Filled With Human Teeth And Seashells"

I would like to thank my teachers: Michael Dickman, Robert Fanning, Maria Mazziotti Gillian, Marie Howe, Dianne Kerr, Chuck Kinder, Thomas Lux, Jack Ridl, and Richard Tillinghast, and my editor, Julie Albright. I am greatly indebted to the members of the poetry workshops to which I belong in Pittsburgh that are headed by Angelle Ellis, Michael Schneider, Laurie Arnold, and Sheila Kelly. I would also like to thank these friends who have always supported my poetic endeavors: Bill Richards, Jim Hutt, Rodger McDaniel, Bob Walaki, Larry Kohler, Elwin Cotman, Joyce Savre, Carl Sharpe, M. L. Liebler, Leah Richards, Bob Walaki, Joan Bauer, Julienne Taylor Michaels, Dale Hull, Gary Metris, Diane Neil, Chuck Neil, Laura Horner, Robert Alexander, Katie Mead, Ariel Brice, Jeannine Shinoda, and the participants and faculty of the Bear River Writers' Conference led by Keith Taylor and Monica Rico. Most of all I would like to thank my wife, the poet Judith Alexander Brice, for her inspiration, support, and love. This book is dedicated to her.

Made in the USA
Middletown, DE
16 April 2016